RAINDROPS

Kai Ilaoa

BookLeaf
Publishing

India | USA | UK

Presentation by *BookLeaf Publishing*

Web: www.bookleafpub.com

E-mail: info@bookleafpub.com

ISBN: 9789363310193

First edition 2024

I dedicate this book to Gerene--my best friend, loving fiancée (and soon to be wife,) my beautiful, tough & tender boi. May I never run out of ways to say I love you.

ACKNOWLEDGEMENT

I want to thank my first teacher, my mother, Susanne McCool Hunkin. You taught me to love poetry by reading aloud Robert Frost on cold winter mornings.

Thank you to every English professor who ever believed in me. I would not be here without you, namely Dr. Suzanne Wolfe and Professor Kelli Worrall.

Special thanks to the beautiful writer Riham Adley for opening up my gifts for the written word after being dormant for so long.

Thank you to Jim and Gale Curtis for guiding me along the woodland path of spirituality and giving me the practical advice I needed.

Thank you to all my favorite poets who kept poetry alive and lush for me—there are too many of you to name, but you are in my blood now. Thank you, Rainier Maria Rilke for saving my life in a Barnes & Noble when I first picked up your Book of Hours.

This collection would not have been possible without the love of my life, Gerene—thank you for believing in me. I love you.

PREFACE

This book is a love letter--to my fiancée, to myself and all my past selves, to all the marginalized LGBTQ+ people who ever felt alone, to those who think they will never find love again, and to those who have found it and know that nothing matters more.

RAINDROPS

Teach me how two raindrops become one
Teach me how they fall into each other--
One and one,
Then two,
then one...
Slipping down the blue veins of a hosta leaf,
Slipping through a thousand fractals of light
before each thunder groan
and lightning strike.
How can they know each other from the clouds
before?
And how do they fall and scatter into more?
When do they rejoin each other again
After running down the cracks of the thirsty
ground,
After flooding between the fractured pavement
to get back to each other?
And when they finally pool together,
In some lake or river or puddle somewhere.
Countless, like teardrops.
How do they know that they will someday rejoin
in the sky?
Atop a mountain?
Upon the cheek of a girl who has started to cry

At the graveside of the woman who planted the
hostas?
Please, teach me how to return, over and over
again
To the sky, to the earth, from the earth, to the
sky.
From myself, to my love, and back again,
Without tearing or breaking or bursting
Instead—flowing, reflecting
Rejoining.
Filling an entire ocean with the love collected
from each time
We lost and found each other.

FLUTTERING

Her eyes like birds,
Fluttered over my body
Hovering over every curve and fold--
Like the spirit over the face of the deep waters
Before everything was called into being.
And I found myself rising,
Waiting like a trembling flower--
For the rain,
For the sun,
For the storm...
Whatever she would bring me.
And instead
she rested her gaze in mine and said
"I love you right now, as you are,"
Forever changing me.

HEAT LIGHTNING

Words I might regret
Falling out of my mouth,
But it's too late to check the weather.
We know it's coming now.
Too late to hold it back,
And I need to be free
Of the wondering and waiting.
Just a few little words
Could change everything,
For better or worse.
Flashing on my lips--
Heat lightning.
At first
You say nothing.
No thunder replies
To the light in my eyes.
I just gave you the power to strike
Come hell or high water.
I need to know what comes next!
Is it rain
Dripping from your mouth to mine?
Is it the storm
Finally ripping the clouds in half?
I've done this before
With too many drinks and too many lovers

Who never deserved half.
The silent air between us feels thick--
Like Iowa summer heat,
Like having no AC and low standards
Naked, leaning out my third story apartment
window
Yelling at the sky.
Break, break, break my heart already!
Or fuck me till I'm dry!
They say if you count between lightning flashes
You can clock how fast the storm is going by.
So I count.
You took a breath.
And I count...
Then you said
The same three words
A thunderclap
Pulsing out of your whole body
Flashing from your lips, pressing into mine,
Too late to go back--
Heat lightning.

A Lesbian's Guide to Eating Mangos

How to eat a mango--
Swollen ripe with the sun
Dripping juice as soon as your knife
Slides across sunrise flesh.
Peeling back green skin,
You would never know how golden it was
inside--
How sweet and tangy
(With notes of cedar trees)
If you never tried.

To pick out a mango,
Ripe for now
Is an art-form nobody can teach you,
Unless you've touched them with
Your own hands...
Your fingers know what to do.
They ask the question:
"Are you ready?"
And you must learn to listen
For the "yes."

Tell the Birds I Love Her

Tell the birds I love her.
Tell them I'm staying right here,
And I will not be flying south for the winter
anymore.
I found someone who keeps me warm,
Not just my body--
But my whole heart.

Tell the trees I love her.
And as the seasons pass
My love only grows deeper
Like the roots of the tree where I sat
And asked her to hold my heart forever...
And she said yes.

SUPERNOVA

I didn't expect it to open me up
To pop me open like champagne and pour me
out all over the floor
I didn't expect you to see everything
immediately come spilling out
I had been hiding so well, so very very well
A star in a human body.

The buildup fizzed inside me, and I thought at
the last second
we should probably stop.
But I didn't want you to stop.
Keep going, keep going, oh god yes like that no
stay like that oh god!

Humans usually cum in liquids.
I came in galaxies, in supernovas, in a molten
lava that erupted from mountains and geysers
that escaped their underground estuaries.
I swirled and eddied and whirled about the
room, drenching everything in whatever the
universe is made of.

Only then did you stop, pause, head limp on my
chest, looking up at me.

I felt more naked than when I had taken off my
clothes.
I covered my eyes,
a splatter of stars on your face, planets and
moons tangled in your hair.
I had marked you forever, and yet you didn't
burn out.
We were supposed to burn out as soon as we hit
earth's atmosphere.
If we hit the ground, we eventually cooled and
became dead rocks.
But here I was, still here, still with you.

"You okay?" You ask, grasping my hand,
soothing the black hole from which you drew
me from,
the nebulas slowly returning to me like lazy
clouds in a summer day.
"I'm sorry, I'm sorry…"

I wiped some Milky Way off your cheek and
started to laugh a little,
tears falling from my eyes like meteors.
You kissed my belly and pulled yourself up
beside me.
"You're perfect," you said, "you're perfect."

I Talked to the Trees About You

And I talked to the trees about you
The minute I felt like running.
My feet got that familiar itch
And tried to pull my heart away.

And the trees asked me,
"Why do you ask for good things
If you don't think you deserve them
when they come to you?"

And I looked out at the lake and smiled,
Because the way the light danced on the water
Reminded me of your eyes,
When you looked at me beneath the canopy of
leaves and sighed
"I wish this could last forever."

And I took a deep breath,
And I called you back.
I was done running from the good things I could
have.

For Doris

No concept of time or space
When every minute is measured
By the sound of someone's breath.
When every hour is passed holding on tight
To that fraying thread we call life.
Living a good life is something we are never
taught,
Let alone dying a good death.
And yet there is no longer containment:
The purple flowers by the old farmhouse.
The yellow rust on the abandoned silo.
The trill of frogs and the flutter of birds--
All the ripples of a life.
It does not end in death,
In one last rattle of one last breath.
It continues in the first cry of a child,
In the laughter of the family members waiting in
the next room.
In the heart of a girl who has finally found love,
Who carries the same stubbornness and
unmoving love as her grandmother.
Maybe it isn't life that stays—
Drawn out to begin again,
To be shared once more with the surrounding
world.

Maybe it's love that stays--
More tangible than hands grasping for
something to hold onto.
Steadier than a heartbeat that is ready to be freed
from the repetition of suffering
Maybe it's love we see when we look at sunset
and whisper "thank you" to all who have gone
before.
No one teaches us how to die a good death,
But maybe love can teach us how to keep living
after life.
Newborn fresh after the rain--
We can go home and begin again.

GREEN

I used to look for love like fire,
Burning quickly and then gone.
Constantly in need of stoking--
Eating up everything to keep it burning.
Let our love be like moss
growing over the trees,
Seeking to make new old things.
Covering everything with a damp softness,
Welcoming every drop of rain and sun.
Covering earth and wood and stone equally.
Blossoming instead of burning.
Bringing new life to the tired earth,
A soft landing for the tired soul--
A green kind of love.

THAWING

Everything is slowly dissolving,
Thawing.
Like the snow on the ground...
Like the lies that we tell ourselves...
Like the old stories that we were frozen into,
Ready to break free.
Let's dissolve, you and me
Into something new.
Like the trees in spring
we are the always changing--
always becoming--
already being.
So let's just be.

SALEM

Not all of us were good girls.
Some of us were witches.
When we wouldn't obey them, they burned us
instead
They couldn't hear the Earth breathing like
us—they couldn't sing hear her songs.
We pressed our ears to her bosom and listened,
Wove our spells with the seasons.
They did not want us to think, to feel, to be
strong.
Honor and obey.
Pray your sins away.
Bad girls, bitches.
Yes, we said the prayers in the daylight,
Then we danced naked in the moonlight,
Under a canopy of stars, we made savage love.
Did we worship the Devil?
Well, if we ever did,
The Devil was much kinder than the God that
wished us dead.
Good girl, good daughter, good mother, good
wife.
Say your prayers or your throat will be slit in
your sleep by the righteous knife.
Some of us hid our spells in the recipes of bread,

Some of us had to keep them safe, under lock
and key, in our heads.
Burning our grimoires, we whispered them to
our children instead,
We tucked our secrets in the songs we sang,
The lullabies that rocked our babies to sleep.
No, we have not gone.
Our magic still lies between the roots of the trees
where we hung.
No, we were not all good girls—
Because in the end, we got on our knees for no
one.

DOOMSCROLLING

The shadows of the trees
Dance across the screen of my phone
Catching my eye, hooked like a fish—

Do fish even know that they're drowning?

Swimming neck-deep in the endless scroll
The current events try to drag me in
But I resist the tide
Until I'm too tired to swim anymore...

Do fish ever tire of swimming?

The trees disappear in the blue-light glow
and I inevitably give in to the pull.

Do fish thirst for more, like me?

Washed out to sea
I'm farther away from you and me
Than I've ever been before...

Do fish know when they are caught?
Line, hook and sinker—landed.
Is it slow? Or quick?
Like the knife that guts them for fish sticks?

HUNGER

I want a burger—
But something that never had a mother.
I don't need my vegan meat to bleed
To find satisfaction in the making.
Non-meat cooks differently:
You have to add moisture,
The fat, the spice.
You have to watch it.
It doesn't take long to burn—
And you can eat it pink without getting sick.
My People eat mostly meat
They don't know what vegan means
Yet they feel close to me when I cook
What is this?
They point, brown fingers
This is not meat
Smoked for hours in a stone pit.
Eat, eat!
No one goes home hungry here
This is not meat—
But it is Home
Warmth, Belonging,
Sustenance.
Laughing around a table cleared away for cards
and coffee,

Dessert always at hand.
Take a plate with you!
No one goes hungry here—
No one is ever alone here.

THE WHALES

I am landlocked but
The whales still call to me.
They swim in my veins
With songs I can't remember in a language I was
never taught,
Pulsing in my ears like ocean waves.
Sometimes it's so loud I can't sleep—
Is this how everyone feels when they first leave
the Islands?
Born in the States, but I still feel
The tropical sun beneath my chest,
The lush green leaves encircling me
Pulling pulling me to go, go, go home.

I sell everything and buy a ticket
I leave my family and I fly alone
My phone set on airplane mode, I ignore
everyone.
"You're crazy, you're not thinking clearly"
But I'm about to cut myself open with a knife to
let the whales go, go, go home.

When I set foot on the soil of my ancestors, the
singing grows louder.

Swelling until I'm vibrating with the echoes of
my forefathers and foremothers.
Someone points in a direction, and I run towards
the glimmering water
Full stop at the shore's edge, eyes straining over
the impossibly blue sea.
They're calling, calling, calling to me.

"What are you looking for, kid?"
A fisherman, curious, says it my native tongue
then in English, the language of our colonizers.
I can barely hear him over the belly-deep roar of
the whales twisting to get out of my head.
"The whales," I finally gasp, " where are the
whales?"
I am frantic, I am sweating, I have not eaten or
drank anything since the flight.
And I feel dizzy—
I want to throw myself in the ocean.

As if he knows, he takes me by the shoulder and
steps me back from the edge.
"We haven't seen the whales here in a long
time," he says.

I fall to my knees and stare out to sea.
A crushed soda can floats next to me, and the
fisherman picks it up, puts it in a bag at his
waist.

"Why you here, manamea?"
I look up at him helplessly, calmly baiting his
hook again, even though there were no fish.
"I can hear them," was all I said…
I couldn't explain.
He nods, a grunt of understanding
His silence is a fishing-line holding me until it's
cast.
Then he asks, "Have you tried singing back?"

TRASH CHUTE

Yesterday I cut you out of my life
Erased you completely, nothing left—
All the photos, the memories, the conversations:
I packed it all and threw it down the trash chute.
Unfortunately, the trash chute got clogged.
I watched the maintenance guy take a broom
handle to it from below.
I didn't feel guilty until my box came tumbling
out on top of our heads—
Shards of sunlight, of storm clouds,
Bits of playlists I compiled for you.
Laughing, moaning, arguing, yelling
And then the silence—
It was the silence that had gotten the whole thing
stuck.
Oozing out of the cardboard box like hot,
bubbling tar under an August sun.
The whole thing was like a horrific no-baked
cookie of regret and sadness,
Of firsts and wishful thinking.
There were chunks of despair in there,
But I ate most of those to get my life back on
track long ago.

I tried to help the poor maintenance man pick up the mess, which was now sticking to the other trash in the chute.
I picked up a snippet of your breakup text—covered in trash juice and bits of food waste.
I caught a glimpse of your picture stuck to someone's cat-shit.
"Who would do this?" He swore, not for the first time.
I cut myself on the text before I could toss it in the dumpster.
I shrugged, trying to play dumb, but the tears were threatening to out me.
"Terrible," I said, adding drops of blood to the mix.
"Nobody cares how their actions impact others anymore."

WINTER

And I see myself less and less nowadays.
Coming and going, we nod and walk by each
other.
Acknowledging, gently, that life is tough.
The winter makes us hunch our shoulders and
walk like someone is chasing us.
I want to be warmer.
Not just with cozy blankets and a cup of tea—
I want to be my own fireside.
I want to be able to sit with myself and read a
good book.
Journal again—without fear or judgement from
the only one who reads it.
I want to be able to make love to myself without
being too tired—
I want to move my hips again,
Like the warm seas in my bloodline.
Iced over, I don't know how to thaw and
refreeze myself without going rotten.
Nothing seems to cut it—
One moment I am one with the universe,
Another colored string in the tapestry.
The next, I am a far-flung rock
Burning out in the atmosphere of my own
self-pressure.

I want to glow instead of sputter.
I feel like my bones are as old as my soul,
And that I can't even look at the birds without
feeling envy for their wings.
I ask the sparrows—
"All your friends have left you!
And you have wings to find the sun down south
again,
So why do you stay?"
The sparrows sing back to me in the cold sharp
air,
"We don't want to miss this:
The sharpness of living,
The warmth of drawing closer,
The blinding blue sky and the stark white snow
against the blood-red berries we savor in our soft
bellies.
The way the water freezes over and still remains
alive underneath,
Until it trickles to life again at first thaw—
This, this, this is why we stay.
To remind the earth that we're still alive,
To remind ourselves with every quick intake of
frosty breath
That we have lungs not just to breathe.

CHERRY COLA

No one had kissed me before that summer—
She smelled like warm soda and lakewater.
Sugary, sweet, vegetative…
To this day
When I drink cherry cola,
I can still taste her.

No one had ever kissed me before—
Just the boy next door,
On a double-dog dare,
A snake in the grass, jumping up to bite me.
I yelled at him, and he ran away laughing.
I don't count that.
No one had kissed me before her.

On the lake, just me and her
We tipped over her father's canoe
Laughing,
Wet, young, wanting
The cherry cola spilled too.
She almost drowned me,
My heart was pounding—
And I don't think she ever knew
She was my first.
No one had ever kissed me before her.

I have tasted many kisses since then:
Some slick with whiskey,
Some heavy red
With wine, or lipstick—I wasn't sure.
To this day
When I drink cherry cola,
I can still taste her.

SOURDOUGH STARTER

One time I tried to make sourdough bread.
But classically, I tried to speed up the process—
Cut corners, find the shortcut to something that
usually takes weeks to build.
Not only that, but I decided to make this
first-time attempt at sourdough artistry for a new
lover.
We had never been in bed yet, and neither had
the sourdough.
Everything should have been given more time.
I think I put too much yeast, not enough flour,
the recipe was bogus (ripped off the internet in a
hurry.
I just wanted to impress,
And eat a hot, buttery slice of fresh, warm
bread--
I wanted to have it all in one night.
A connection that's cared for over time
Like sourdough, you feed it and nurture it until it
grows and deepens in flavor,
Until it oozes with the richness of its time
resting and being.
I suppose I wanted a relationship
(Even though I said I was "just dating")

The dough didn't rise right, but I still stuck it in
the oven.
It reeked like vinegar, but I still popped it in,
with a wish and a prayer, and set a timer
The sex wasn't good.
I kept thinking the bread was burning
(Who thinks about their bread burning while
they're supposed to be swept away in the throes
of a passionate encounter?)
It had been too long in the oven,
It should be done by now…
I popped up (in the middle of everything)to
check on it.
Scorched and burnt and still reeking of
something that hadn't been carefully planned or
thought through.
I apologized--
To the lover, to the bread, to myself.
That's when I should have chucked everything
in the trash and went home.
I haven't made any sourdough since then--
I have been nervous to even make any kind of
bread for you.
Until today, when I caught a waft of a whim,
And it felt good to take my time, to know that I
could do this.
To know that what we have lasts because it's fed,
nurtured
Slowly over time...

Risen to perfection, and then baked off,
Yielding golden pieces of soft clouds we can
tear off and butter at our leisure.

GRIT

Everyone wants the smooth stone--
The water wending softly through the forest.
The summer breeze.
I'm tired of being the smoother,
The peacemaker--
I want to be the grit.
The rough edges.
The catalyst of change.
The sand that makes smooth the roughest stones.
The torrential waterfall that carves glaciers and
canyons
With fury and thunder and lightning.
I want to carve my name into the walls of sacred
caves
They find years later--
Lasting centuries of wind and weather.
They will see the symbols and wonder
How the stones grew so smooth?
It wasn't the voiceless that lasted, the
peacemaker, the passive.
It was the trouble-makers, the survivors--
I want to be the problem.
I want to be the entire roaring volcano
Engulfing Pompeii in flames.
I want to burn it all down and start again.

I want to be the mountain you have to climb to
reach the stars.

Interabled Couple

Answering the drumbeat of my heart
I dance with you.
"But how can you dance with someone
whose feet don't touch the ground?" they ask.
I smile in surprise,
For we have danced by the sun,
Made love by the moon,
And not once did I ever think anything was
lacking in me or you.
I have to be reminded
That my eyes hold you in a circle of roses.
When I look at you, I see all of you.
I just see two lovers dancing in the kitchen
Late on a Saturday night.
Our dance-steps are different,
But the song is the same song I heard through
the trees
When you first asked me to dance with you
forever.

PRELUDE: A Blessing

35

May you find a soft resting place for your wild
soul,
Somewhere they won't build you a gilded cage
and call it love.
Somewhere you can choose to come and go,
Somewhere so beautiful you choose to stay and
linger
Long after the snow melts,
And the flowers begin to grow.